Famous Lives

The Life of George Washington

By Maria Nelson

Gareth Stevens Publishing

Please visit our website, www.garethstevens.com. For a free color catalog of all our high-quality books, call toll free 1-800-542-2595 or fax 1-877-542-2596.

Library of Congress Cataloging-in-Publication Data

Nelson, Maria.
The life of George Washington / Maria Nelson.
p. cm. — (Famous lives)
Includes index.
ISBN 978-1-4339-6351-3 (pbk.)
ISBN 978-1-4339-6352-0 (6-pack)
ISBN 978-1-4339-6349-0 (library binding)
1. Washington, George, 1732-1799—Juvenile literature. 2. Presidents—United States—Biography—Juvenile literature. I. Title.
E312.66.N44 2012
973.4'1092—dc23
[B]

2011020900

First Edition

Published in 2012 by
Gareth Stevens Publishing
111 East 14th Street, Suite 349
New York, NY 10003

Designer: Daniel Hosek
Editor: Kristen Rajczak

Photo credits: Cover, pp. 1, 5, 7, 17, 21 Stock Montage/Getty Images; pp. 9, 15 Hulton Archive/Getty Images; pp. 11, 13 MPI/Getty Images; p. 19 Buyenlarge/Getty Images.

Printed in the United States of America

CPSIA compliance information: Batch #CW12GS: For further information contact Gareth Stevens, New York, New York at 1-800-542-2595.

Contents

Boldface words appear in the glossary.

Founding Father

George Washington served as the first president of the United States. He led the **colonial** army during the **American Revolution**. He was known throughout the world as an honorable man and important leader.

Early Life

George was born in 1732 to a **wealthy** Virginia family. His father died when George was 11. George then lived part of the time with his mother and part of the time with his oldest brother at Mount Vernon.

In 1752, George joined the Virginia **militia**. He led it during a war between France and England that began in 1754. George became well respected. In 1759, he married Martha Dandridge Custis. They lived at Mount Vernon.

Revolution!

By the 1760s, the colonies were unhappy with British rule. In 1774, **representatives** from all the colonies met in Philadelphia, Pennsylvania. George represented Virginia. He shared his views on many matters.

The American Revolution began in 1775. George was chosen to lead the colonial army. He was strong and brave during the war. George's battle plans helped the colonists win their freedom!

Making a Country

George returned to Philadelphia in 1787. There, he led the meeting at which the **US Constitution** was written. It stated that the country's leader would be a president chosen by the people.

The First President

George became the first US president in 1789. He was so well liked that he was voted into office again in 1792. George worked to gain other countries' respect for the United States.

An Honorable Man

George died on December 14, 1799. People all over the world honored him. Friend Henry Lee wrote that George was "first in war, first in peace, and first in the hearts of his countrymen."

Remembering George

Today, George Washington is remembered in many ways. Washington, DC, and the state of Washington are named for him. The Washington Monument was built in his honor. We even celebrate George's birthday!

Timeline

- **1732** — George is born.
- **1754** — George leads the Virginia militia.
- **1759** — George marries Martha.
- **1775** — George leads the army during the American Revolution.
- **1789** — George is elected president.
- **1799** — George dies.

Glossary

American Revolution: the war in which the American colonies won their freedom from England

colonial: having to do with colonies, which are lands under the control of another country

militia: a group of people who only fight when needed

representative: a person who stands for a group of people

US Constitution: the piece of writing that states the laws of the United States

wealthy: rich

For More Information

Books

Catel, Patrick. *Key People of the Revolutionary War.* Chicago, IL: Heinemann Library, 2011.

Ransom, Candice F. *George Washington and the Story of the U.S. Constitution.* Minneapolis, MN: Millbrook Press, 2011.

Websites

Name That Founding Father

www.history.org/kids/games/foundingFather.cfm
Play a game to learn more about the Founding Fathers.

Rediscovering George Washington

www.pbs.org/georgewashington
Read more about George Washington.

Publisher's note to educators and parents: Our editors have carefully reviewed these websites to ensure that they are suitable for students. Many websites change frequently, however, and we cannot guarantee that a site's future contents will continue to meet our high standards of quality and educational value. Be advised that students should be closely supervised whenever they access the Internet.

Index